DAD JOKES FROM LATE IN
THE PATRIARCHY

Sundress Publications • Knoxville, TN

Editor: Jeremy Michael Reed
Editorial Assistant: Kanika Lawton
Editorial Interns: Lee Anderson, Eliza Browning, Hannah Soyer

Colophon: This book is set in Bembo Std and Century Gothic.

Cover Design: Kristen Ton

Book Design: Erin Elizabeth Smith

DAD JOKES FROM LATE IN THE PATRIARCHY
Amorak Huey

CONTENTS

For Zoe-Kate & Eli —

You can pick your nose,
but you can't pick your dad,
& you sure can't pick your dad's nose.

Like it or not, all my jokes are for you.

SETUPS

A Primer

My complaint about life is it happens
only in order: a thesis of sorts,

a kind of argument
that might seem out of place here.

But I have seen a man ride his bicycle
into beltline traffic & die.

I have seen my grandmother coughing blood
after a lifetime of menthols.

I have seen the closed casket of a friend
who asked the wrong person

for a ride home after a long shift.
The end of a story

is the shape of a hole in the fence
the story runs through

on its way to the end.
Spielberg filmed *E.T.*

in chronological order
so his young cast could deliver

an authentic emotional performance;
it helped them bond with the alien

in the natural course of the narrative,
leading to the weepy climax

he sought. This anecdote suggests
something about art, youth, loss;

something about believability. Or
the cruelty of a man who knows what he wants.

Pa & Michael Landon & Buddy Ebsen
& Daniel Boone

He moves through dark woods, checking traps & splitting logs. The work of keeping a family alive against another long winter. The cruelty needed to survive & no more; the particular gracelessness of a thin man with a large beard. A caught fox screams. Or a rabbit. Because blood needs blood. Because a man has a duty. My father moves, then moves again. America is fond of its rootless men. I walk beside. I carry a bow & arrow. I do not know how to shoot. He will not ask for help. He teaches me the names of blackbirds, the songs of trees. How to peel back bark & tap the sugar beneath. I imagine such sweetness, a cold wind. We stand & press on in the deepening snow.

Fairy Tale

after Tanya Grae

I cannot wear my father's body—
we are a poor fit—

as my son will not
wear mine, now

or ever. To feel myself pinned
between the two boulders

of my body & my duty.
To always be the one leaving,

never the left behind—
such language

has the ring of truth
which resembles

a wedding ring
which resembles

the corona around the sun
on the day I've chosen

to drop my children
in the woods—

so many stories
end with a man

watching a trail
of bread crumbs

disappear & not
knowing how to feel.

There are so many
names for God;

if they rhyme with *father*
you're saying them wrong.

We Were All Odysseus in Those Days

A young man learns to shoot
& dies in the mud
an ocean away from home,
a rifle in his fingers
& the sky dripping
from his heart. Next to him
a friend watches
his final breath slip
ragged into the ditch,
a thing the friend will carry
back to America—
wound, souvenir,
backstory. He'll teach
literature to young people
for 40 years. He'll coach
his daughters' softball teams.
Root for Red Wings
& Lions & Tigers. Dance
well. Love generously.
He'll be quick with a joke
& firm with handshakes.
He'll rarely talk
about the war. If asked
he'll tell you instead
his favorite story:
Odysseus escaping
from the Cyclops
with good wine, a bad pun
& a sharp stick.

It's about buying time
& making do, he'll say.
It's about doing what it takes
to get home, & you see
he has been talking
about the war all along.
We all want the same thing
from this world:
Call me nobody. Let me live.

Ward Cleaver & Mike Brady & Fred MacMurray & Dick Van Patten

A man brings his work home. He shows up at the end of the day to dole out discipline & eat meatloaf, to fix bicycles & assign blame. Briefcase. Strong hands. A love of puns. I imagined my parents' childhood in black & white, playing out in two-act structure on a wooden console in the living room. Get into hot water, get out. TV trays & bottles of Coke, live studio audience & a happy ending. A million cigarettes. My friends' parents were unhappy & I did not know why. My parents were unhappy & I thought I knew why. I learned the wrong lessons from every episode. Now it is early evening. I'm standing next to my father on the front porch. He slings his coat over his shoulder. He loosens his tie. The porch swing creaks in the wind, rusted chain grinding. We are actors. We are characters. We have not rehearsed what happens next.

Elegy for What I Want to Be When I Grow Up

My father spent three years in his workshop
making cities to sell. They fed us,
these lean haunted cedarscapes
angled against imagined hills.
Windows dark like eyes. Jigsaw-cut
wood-glued tenements,
elaborate deceptions
in the last days of my parents' marriage.
I learned to bat left-handed,
thinking it would mean something
eventually. Wrong, of course.
I will never have that kind of control
over my body. That call
to the majors increasingly unlikely
as I zigzag toward 50. Blame genetics—
not born with enough fast-twitch
muscle fiber—or desire.
Blame the unhappy childhood
I did not have for my lack
of hunger. Enough
to keep me alive, no more.
I expected to be a protagonist,
to be good with my hands,
to have a better haircut, maybe.
To be the maker, not the made.
Expected pallets of shingles
stacked outside my adult life
waiting to be transformed. I
would draw the plans,

do the work: Walls.
Windows. Everything else
up to my imagination.

Fred Flintstone & George Jetson

I am somewhat embarrassed to admit where I've gotten most of my ideas about how the world works & am definitely embarrassed to admit how much time I spend thinking about people who have more money than I do. When I was thirteen, my mother said, *You want to be one of the beautiful people*, & although I knew she didn't mean it as a compliment, I took it that way. I did not realize it was already too late, this is a club you're in or you're not. I did not realize I had invented the club myself & the main requirement is that you must be not me. I thought it would be enough to break rocks or build sprockets & to zip home at the end of the day to give my wife a hard time about how much she had shopped that afternoon, & although now that I write this down, it obviously seems vapid & unsatisfying, I knew early this was the model. What I wanted to be when I grew up? Someone who has a dishwasher, a riding mower, a fickle boss to complain about, & so on, & now all these years later I have or have had most of these things, & still I live across the street from the backsides of the houses where the beautiful people come out on summer evenings to grill steaks & caviar on their custom-built outdoor kitchens; sometimes I can hear them laughing, possibly at the poor sap who lives across the street & thinks you grill caviar, who believes in the nobility of hard work, who thinks that if you break enough rocks, surely you will open a path out of the quarry.

Fairy Tale

We built a barn. Populated it.
Three goats, thirty chickens, a pig.
Waited for them to speak,
naturally. We hoped to be told
what to do next. Or possibly
to be granted a wish. We waited
a long time. No one spoke.
We pretended to leave,
listened at the door. Nothing.
We left for the night,
tiptoed back at sunrise.
Nothing. Nothing. Nothing.
Thus, our lives proceeded.
My parents divorced. My
father moved off the farm.
One by one, the animals
died. Nothing surprising
or cruel, merely the way life
goes in the end. It's not profound,
it simply is: what lives, dies.
My mother moved. My brother
& I were long gone.
The barn stood quiet for years.
When it came down,
it did so gradually. I cannot
recall what we would have
wished for. It doesn't matter.
The possibility of the wish
always meant more

than the substance.
It lasted a while. It was
a place to leave. This,
in the end, is all we could ask.

In the Final Months of My Parents' Marriage

We are building a flying machine, my father, my brother,
& me. We work in the attic of an abandoned house—

to reach this room, we lean the rusting skeleton
of a box spring against the wall & heave our bodies up

through a trap door. Wood glue, balsa, complicated
mimeograph blueprint—it's a kit from the Farm & Feed,

a gift, a getaway vehicle; although none of us
knows it yet, we are each in our own separate hurries

away from this place. The work is delicate, requires
a kind of care I've never had. They are both better

than I am at this; if it were left to me, I would crack
these thin slices of wood, render them useless.

Down the hill, a chert driveway, crushed stone
& packed sand. Across the road, a field. Beyond that,

behind a row of scrub pine & water oak, a river.
But today it's the field we need. An open space

to test our work. A rubber band. A winding tight.
A letting go & a grassy place to land.

Steven Keaton & Dan Conner & Bob Saget & Alan Thicke & Both of My Two Dads

Well-meaning but befuddled, that's how we find ourselves in a house slightly too big for its occupants. A surprise fourth child, an apron to wear at the grill. All this smoke & we're overcooking everything. No one wants raw meat. *Don't kill the family* is the only rule that's written down. Everything else we're supposed to sense. Not that it's brain surgery. Some of us are better at disappearing into the role. Imagine having to act like this all the time. Imagine it's the only thing people will remember you for. Every day you get dressed up & sound out the first sentence of your obituary. On our walk after dinner, one of my fathers & I find a dead raccoon. *Can I take the tail?* I ask. He hands me a knife. He says, *Cut as close as possible to the body.*

Fairy Tale

My father cuts off his thumb with a circular saw.
A tiny magical man makes me an offer

I cannot refuse. My father's thumb grows back.
The price I have agreed to pay is too great,

I cannot bear to say its name aloud. In the corner
of every room I enter, the tiny magical man

crouches, nameless & cruel. *Not today*, he says.
Not today. One day, I will enter a room & he will

not be there & I will know the bill has come due.
A phone will ring. I will answer. A stranger's voice

will mispronounce my name, apologize,
hesitate. In this brief silence, foolish hope will bloom.

I Am Not Arnold Schwarzenegger

I am fourteen years old at the video store deciding on a movie my father & brother might both enjoy, deciding who I will be for the rest of my life; oh how this can go wrong; there are so many rules that I'm grateful for any that are written down: Rewind. Return by noon. Three movies per night per household, more than enough for the forty-eight hours we have to fill each week. Choice after choice, & every story promises the same metaphors for the cold war, or sex, or the war between the sexes, all of which is shorthand for adults not understanding each other, or themselves; I haven't learned this yet, I still believe wisdom is real & waiting around the corner. I want to see *Porky's* but my father is in the car & I'm not supposed to know about the skin mags in the back of his desk; we keep our erections to ourselves. We watched *Risky Business* on last weekend's visit & I would happily spend two more hours with Rebecca De Mornay, but my father doesn't like the ending. *Terminator*, then. Again. It's no longer a surprise when Arnold turns out to be the villain, but still. There's pleasure in watching him learn to be human so he can destroy us. His body is a marvel. A measure against which I have no chance. His body is relentless. I am somehow both skinny & pudgy. His biceps are a religion. My bones are only bone. No titanium anywhere. I am too young to see the inevitability of a sequel in which he is the hero. *Sarah Connor?* Arnold asks, his eyes hidden behind those sunglasses, & I see what he's really asking. *Yes*, I want to say, *yes, I am*, though I know what the answer will cost.

Looking At Men
after Iliana Rocha

The world teaches us there's nothing to see here,
only everything that matters. The world
teaches us to fear what desires us: a matter
of survival. The world's pedagogy
has not evolved lately, all armpit hair & biceps
& bigger is better. Doesn't matter
if a man's wearing a three-piece that costs more
than your car or a neon vest or a prison jumpsuit,
he has a right to the space you occupy.

A memory: junior-high baseball tryouts,
this boy making fun of my name.
He was a running back & special-teams star,
fast & strong & angry all the time,
popular & dangerous; he'd die of heart failure
at forty-two but of course we didn't know that.
On this day all that mattered was that we both knew
he would be the starting center fielder
once he'd finished shredding me. It's how
things work. How they have always worked.
When I tried ignoring him, willing myself
invisible & mute, he dropped his glove
& jogged toward me, spitting profanity.
We were boys but he saw what it meant
to be a man: no problem aggression
can't solve, flex & fist, cock & rock
& stomp out weakness. I did not make
the team that year, or the next.

In porn, the men are supposed to be
invisible—who wants to focus on that dangle
& flop & hairy flesh—women are the centerpiece—
& yet it is the men whose pleasure matters,
whose erection lets us know it's time to begin,
whose ejaculation lets us know what success
looks like. This is what the world teaches us,
& I'm exempt from nothing. I love muscles
swelling under sleeves. A beer gut
means you make the rules; hairy forearms
are a ticket to all the backrooms in all the land.

Another junior-high memory: selecting
the yearbook who's who, most likely to
& all that. Asked to vote for best-looking guy,
I picked the starting quarterback,
a dark-haired boy who treated me with contempt.
He was taller than I, stronger, a better athlete,
at ease on the planet. Once I sat behind him
in the bleachers at a high school game while he made out
with a dance-squad girl. She caught me watching,
smirked *Do you have a problem?* Well, sure,
who doesn't, but of course I said nothing,
looked away, chastened & hungry. It was her
I wanted but him I envied. There is zero chance
this man remembers me, but here I am:
not being him still shapes what I think of myself.

I cannot believe how stupid I am. I cannot believe
I'm more than halfway through with this life

& still molded out of ninth-grade humiliations.
I do not dare to admit weakness. I cannot
tell the truth about want. I am not
this body. I am not this sex. I am not
strong enough to be anything else.

Captain Picard Teaches My Son to Throw a Football

Picard is talking about visualization. Imagine the ball leaving your fingers, he says, imagine spin, trajectory, destination. Then make it so. My son rolls his eyes. He just wants to throw. Kirk was a way better captain, he says. My son values deed over word. My son believes in kicking problems in the face. Picard is unbothered, tireless. His example toss transcribes a perfect helix. Everything he says contains multiple layers of wisdom. He describes the route he will run, tells my son to count to four before firing to the outside shoulder. Down, set, engage, he says. My son's throw hits Picard in the back of the head. The spiral, the bald spot, the ball bouncing away. The lesson proceeds.

Elegy for Dr. Spock

My parents grew up wanting to be told they were loved. I wanted air conditioning & a store-bought haircut. I guess everyone's childhood is fucked. The current president is president of all of us because his father was an approval-withholding asshole. The previous president's father abandoned him early. The president before that was the son of a goddamn president—how unfair is that to everyone involved? The president before that, another absent father. What the hell do we do to our sons? For years, American parents were told not to hug their boy children after they turned five. I like to think I've already eighty-sixed my son's chances of ruling the free world someday, but the moral arc of the patriarchy is long & bends toward most of the damage has already been done.

REINFORCEMENTS

Nocturne with Overdue Books

One of us lies awake, the other sleeps, dreams, both,
we've been at this for years,
it's that kind of marriage. The king bed is new,
what to do with so much space,
the neighbors are new & so young

they cannot hold still
like the mylar balloon tied to the tire swing in their yard,

so red & so shiny, forgive me.

Our kids are still awake in rooms nearby,
laughing at whatever the world's beaming
into their earbuds. It's easy to picture:

beauty in their faces, ghost-glow of handheld screens,
they're alive in the future already
but we will not be.

I forgot to tell you, the library called again today.
We're out of renewals. It's not a metaphor.
I don't know where the books are. Maybe
there's one under the bed.

If this does not sound like a love poem you're reading it wrong.

When a Poet Writes *Afterward* You Know It Means

after having sex;
or, after someone has died.
Before such a thing, or during,
who has time for poetry?
It's April in Michigan, which means
we have plenty of time
& this poem isn't coming
after anything except more
stupid snow. It must
have been a day like this one
when my parents decided
to leave this state, move south,
start over: what hunger
carried them along that highway.
How young they must have felt,
or how old, how purposeful.
They are both still alive,
still in the South, but divorced
& I have nothing meaningful
to say about any of that,
for now. Somehow here I
am, back in this state as if
by accident, twice the age they were,
thinking about you, thinking about
desire, thinking about the tricks
a tongue plays with words,
with weather, with another tongue:
such roads we travel in each other's mouths.

The Song & Dance Comic Teaches Method Acting

Tonight's lesson is called "Aluminum Powder in the Lungs."
Tonight's backstory concerns doing a favor for a friend,

concerns plunging your head into a drum of acid,
concerns being typecast as a sidekick.

Say, "I refuse to sign a long-term contract with your studio."
Say, "What is the name of this ridiculous script?"
Name it: "Tin Doesn't Rust, Assholes."

Abandoned husband, patriarch, clown,
         hero of the Alamo—
everyone dies. Everyone dies of the same thing.

Still Life with Laugh Track

There is one more thing I should tell you about myself.
I'm in the midst of a project
involving wood glue, screws,
the comfort of a hammer.
I am better with my hands than you think I am.

Our cabinets in pieces.
Your naked skepticism.

I haven't been reading enough but the laundry is done.
My brother says the most important part of any job
is having the proper tools.
My muscles forget but my bones remember.

Last night it hailed like the fall of Rome.
Our evening plans canceled
by lightning, I began work. There

is a possibility you will be correct in the end. Imagine

we are in an episode of that show you enjoy.
My line. A beat. Your rebuttal. Canned laughter rising.

FMK

You can leave me & I will not kill you.
That this needs to be said is insane
but I am a man, & this is the world.
Probably it should've been in our vows:
in sickness & so forth,
I will wash your coffee cups
& do the laundry if you fold,
I will walk the dog when it's my turn,
& I will not kill you,
nor will I ever fill your car
with wet cement, which is a thing
I read about today: a man hurt
when a woman declined
to wear his name.
When we married, you kept
your name; people told me
I should be bothered. People
told you that you were young
& did not understand
how the world worked. By people
it should be obvious I mean men.
I don't want to make a joke
of all these wounded
walking around among us
dividing the world
into Fuck Marry Kill,
which is supposed to be
a fun conversation starter
but the world reminds us

over & over there's nothing
funny about it. For every
man who loves you
there are eleven who love you
& will still come to your job
& shoot you in the head.
For every body you have,
there is a man willing to claim it,
one way or another.
The story goes that God
spent five days making
this amazing place, its cedar trees
& canyons & its many egrets
taking flight over many
grassy marshes, & then
on the sixth day he created
men. If God is reading
this poem, if God truly
sees all & knows all,
he's probably thinking,
At least the shorebirds are lovely,
& I have to give him that
even though out there
right now some man
is thinking, *Fuck the shorebirds,*
marry the canyons, kill
everything else. This is the world,
in which, somehow, you
& I found ourselves together,
& in which we wake up
every morning & pledge

not to harm each other
any more than we have already.

The Seventh Anniversary Is Salt & I Do Not Know the Gift for That

I have little to offer. I am not good with my hands.
Here, take these words I did not invent
& cannot sing but have used
in this particular order
for what may or may not be the first time.
I am not the strong silent type, being
neither strong nor silent. Which is good,
because look how many Marlboro Men
died of lung cancer or emphysema.
What doesn't kill you, unless it does, & so forth.
Your former boyfriend once carved you
the head of a lion out of a tree stump
with a chainsaw. Your father writes
you a check every year. Your mother
knits you a new umbilical cord.
I have so much to live up to.
It's a good thing we moved
so far away, then moved again.
This is the life we imagined, a self–
sufficient farm with eggs enough to sell,
two boys naked in the yard & no one
telling us what to do. One of us will stop
smoking, then the other, then both
will stop again, again, again.
We're doing the best we can,
quit looking at us like that.
Obviously we're not from
around here. We chose this place.

Together. It stands for something—
a lawn to call our own, a field
for planting, Muscadine arbor
& gnarled peach tree. We could
grow things here. It's what we wanted.
As a species we are notorious
for not knowing what we want.
We thought ourselves an exception,
but so does everyone &
there aren't any. I think I had
myself confused with my father.
He would know what to do here.
He would see the end coming
& head it off. When I think
about him now, I imagine him
shoveling our driveway in the snow,
spreading a layer of salt to melt the ice
& keep us safe, his family,
because it was his duty & because,
I imagine, he loved us. He smoked
a lot, until he was hit by a truck
& died a few months after he retired
to a city on a gulf, a half-mile from water.
It should not have ended that way
but I guess most of us have such a complaint.
I am probably still not myself—
one of my sons, or both, or some
version of myself I've invented
from television characters
& game show hosts. I am so tired
& still I have nothing to show

for all the hours of my life.
We are miles inland but the air
is dense with saltwater, our
tongues slick with brine.

You're All Why Are We Here & I'm All Because of Sex & You're All You're Not as Funny as You Think You Are & I'm All I'm Not Joking

I have no right to this grief. It's not my body. It's not my body.

It's not my body, not my blood, not my body. I cannot contain

any of this grief. I read that vampire squids live forever

but it's not true unless eight to ten years is forever. Sometimes

an hour is forever, if it's the wrong hour.

I read that their bodies are covered with light-producing organs.

I read that no one has observed their mating process.

Yet they reproduce. Imagine what they might read

about our habits. They are not good

at changing their skin color. It doesn't matter

in the lightless depths. I cannot contain my own body. I am not

good at any of this. I am finding pieces of my grief

all over the yard. This is one definition of faith.

There's a joke about whom an atheist talks to during orgasms—

I can't remember the punchline
        but I'm asking: give me another chance.

The World as We Have Invented It

is a house without blinds or curtains,
as though someone has freshly moved in,
dishes in boxes & clothes in folded piles
in the corners of rooms. Sunlight
everywhere. The insistence, outside,
of a large truck in reverse. One hundred
dogs barking. The slap & drag
of passing joggers on the sidewalk.
I cannot shake the sense
that we do not belong here, surely
we are house sitting for someone
with a claim on such grandeur.
My dreams are like this, sometimes,
a kind of calm, a kind of doubt—
to reach this place, we've traveled
a highway lined with billboards about Jesus,
warning of hell, suggesting it's past time
to take action in regards to salvation.
Certain neighbors visit for a slice of pie;
others happen by to proselytize,
& I mean the ones with that yard sign:
a blown-up photo of a fetus above
an easy hashtag. Sure, I'll sign
your petition to make the world
a better place. But I will also stand
nude at the window, certain no one
cares enough to glance in my direction.
I wake each morning in this world & feel
the weight of the absence where your body belongs.

The World Is Full of Dogs Without Collars
—The New York Times, April 18, 2016

Not quite pets; not quite strays.
We could learn a thing or two
about scavenging, surviving: what it takes
to get though winter. The colder the climate,
the larger the dog. In the tropics, it says,
all dogs are medium-weight & the color of a lion.
I'm going to bed earlier & earlier this spring,
you're drinking more wine, the dishes
are piling up. No. The dishes are fine.
The beds are made, the laundry folded.
One of us is playing the piano, one of us listening.
There's tea in the pot. We've shaped our chaos
into something of a life. The dogs'
most salient power: they can persuade
humans to feed them. This is adaptation.
This is how a living thing stays living.
The origin of dogs remains a mystery;
some ancient hunter probably did not
kidnap & train a wolf. That version sounds
like truth because it affirms our role
as necessary to how the world happens,
but let's face it. You lie less than I do,
but better. Tomorrow we'll learn how
serious we are about our vows. The quicker
one learns to eat a rotten melon, the better
because nothing else was ever promised.
The number of dogs in a city is determined
by the available garbage. The opposite is true of us.

Nocturne in Third Person Plural

They speak occasionally. Not as often
as they should, if *should* is the kind
of word they think, which it is,
they feel a tremendous obligation,
which is to say guilt, but guilt
is a terrible motivator, no one
does anything with guilt but drown in it.
When they speak it is often
about books, basketball, birds
they have seen; it is about what grows
in their yards, which is not the same
because they are so far apart,
one climate spawning daffodils
by the end of February, the other
still muddy with snow as April
crawls into view. When they speak
they laugh & only once in a while
is it too loud. Politics? A rare burst
of shared outrage now & then.
It subsides. All passions fade,
or so they have come to believe.
They disagree on almost nothing
but see the world as if
from opposite ends of a kaleidoscope.
What they do not talk about? I'm sorry,
it's hard for me to say. Maybe
a house, a red one, small,
tucked between two enormous cedars,
this house & the time before

it burned, the house & the time
& the people who lived there,
the farm that surrounded it,
so much that grew there
but the house burned, yes,
& the parents divorced
& the boys moved away,
the house is gone, yes,
& their phone call is at its end,
but there's a kind of peace,
if that's the right word, which it is,
a peace that descends like gauze
as they disconnect.

Good for Food & Pleasing to the Eye, & Also Desirable for Gaining Wisdom

So fucking weird that other people have sex,
someone somewhere orgasming hard
though my god it's six in the morning
and the bedroom is so hot. We would never,
not in these bodies. I woke up early
and watered your geraniums. Yes, yes,
this sounds like a euphemism for making love,
a phrase itself a sloppy portrait
of two bodies tangled in each other's hunger.
We don't have words for most of what we mean,
besides hunger's got nothing to do with it. Do you
remember being twenty-four together?
So much sweat. Call a cockroach a palmetto bug
all you want, there's a reason Florida's
no place for the middle part of a marriage.
We drove to Missouri, to Kentucky, to Michigan,
touching each other the whole way
and if we did not die on those highways
we took it as a promise we'd live forever.
Such recklessness we unlocked in each other,
we thought we'd invented love & lust,
born fully formed into the garden of 1994,
each of us the other's overripe plum,
forgive us our bruises, our smeary faces,
no one else had ever tasted the way
we tasted each other. Who knew
that all these years later
our middle-aged skin would still hold

all the humidity of that season;
how else to talk about that cottage
at Cape San Blas where we played
strip crazy eights & you asked me
to shave you? How my blood storms
at the memory. Don't tell me such sweetness
doesn't come from inside the body.
Don't tell me my desire is a trap.

The Girl on the Unicycle

My life has led me to a one-way street
lined with two-story houses
across from much larger homes
& a neighbor girl riding a unicycle
which she does with no particular grace
but a great deal of earnestness.
A skunk has died under someone's porch.
It's a thing to talk about. The carcass
is gone but the odor lingers—
for how long? we all wonder.
My life is one out-of-body experience
after another. Another neighbor
offers a beer; we talk about our kids,
he is younger than I am
but seems more comfortable here.
His wife grew up a few miles
from where we stand
& babysat the children
of our local grocery magnate.
Everyone starts somewhere;
my life has not stopped feeling
like practice for some life
that's around the corner.
She is not practicing for anything,
the girl on the unicycle,
she is not performing,
she is learning to disappear
into the ride: there is only
this single wheel

against the sidewalk,
& effort, & balance,
& maybe something like pleasure.

MISDIRECTIONS

Thought Experiment

A bare stage, say. A guitar
on scuffed black planks.
The auditorium emptied.
Introduce a subject to this scene.
Man. Woman. Anyone
with all the mercury & blood
of a human being, such
unpredictability. How long
before the subject disorders music?
Discovers, we mean.
It's an experiment
only if there's failure. Silence.
Doubt. Wonder.
These are the components
of the guitar. But first
our subject must reckon
with time. An audience
would change everything.
cast uncertainty on
our results. So our subject
must learn alone to count
by setting fingers on fire
one at a time. After weeks
of ignoring the guitar
the subject crawls over.
The first sounds are far more
urgent than we predicted.
Our methodology did not account
for ... for what? Something

to do with flame, something
to do with the body. There's no
way to anticipate every outcome.
The subject. The stage. The guitar.
Anything beyond that is
outside the scope. Our own
presence fucks up everything.

Road Trip

Sometimes I think about telling the truth
but it doesn't last. Sometimes I think
about the wolves we saw at the edge
of the highway on our drive west
that summer, their heads low,
eyes reflecting our headlights
back at us. At that convenience
store outside Tupelo we bought
a porn mag. You read the classifieds
to me as I drove: couples seeking,
singles seeking, everyone seeking
afraid to say exactly what
though it's pretty clear what
we're talking about.
We laughed at the foolishness
of desire, & got turned on,
& stopped for the night
at 3 in the afternoon. The next
morning, back on the road before sunrise,
is when we saw the wolves.
It felt like an omen. But of what?
That was twenty-three years ago,
half my lifetime, & we lasted
seven months after that trip. My fault
all the way around. I'm still
deciding which pieces
of this story matter most,
which I've got wrong, which I've
forgotten. Was it merely

that we listened to Whitesnake's
"Still of the Night" & imagined
the wolves? No, they were
real. They ignored us, surely,
is how I remember it, & of course
those wolves must all be dead now,
though I have no idea how long
wolves live. Maybe it's forever.

A Dog Barks, Someone Eats a Watermelon, a Car Drives Away

—Edan Lepucki, on how writers mark the passage of time

Say one of us is a supervillain now, or a reluctant hero, or both of us are writing novels we pretend are not about each other. What if every minivan on every avenue carries a different version of this story? So much desire carpooling around unexpressed. Character motivation & the passage of time, that's all you need to understand. We cannot be the people we were. A watermelon will not eat itself. One of us needs to walk the dog. We're each driving away in an Odyssey with high mileage & personalized plates. There are two versions of our love story. One in which you are a prequel, a minor-but-canonical adventure from my past that explains how I turned out this way. One in which the roles are reversed.

Yes, And

If I say everything is a gun
you have to say yes, and

the gun is always going off.
If I say someone could get hurt,

you have to say yes, and
that's what it means to be alive.

I say, does it have to be
like that? You say yes, and

if you had a dime for every
broken heart in your wake,

you could be elected president.
I say, but—and you interrupt:

no arguing. Someone really
could get hurt. Why, only today

some guy shot his wife.
Yes, and he killed a kid, too,

though that might have been
accidental. I say nothing.

You say yes, and let's start again:
It's America. Everything is a gun.

Prayer for What I Do Not Want

I do not want to write a poem about a tyrant. A tyrant is not a poem. Is not a form of a poem. Is not syllable count or metrical pattern. Is not a swarm of bees wearing a poem-suit. Is not one wolf standing on the shoulders of another wolf wearing a trench coat & pretending to be a poem. I do not want to write a poem about men in suits, or wolves in suits, or sheep in cargo shorts. I do not want to write poems about videos of men in suits shooting children or other men. I do not want to write poems about suits of body armor or tear gas. I do not want my poems to be tear gas. I do not want to be tear gassed. I do not want to tear up the documents of our nation's history: declarations & proclamations & constiwhatnots. A nation is not a poem, but each poem is a nation. I believe in words & the opposite of words. I was taught to believe what I was told. I was told to believe in words delivered by mailmen and pastors and presidents. I was told to believe in the power of the simple sentence, delivered with passion and honor by a man in a suit. Or a man standing on the shoulders of other men, wearing a bloody suit of flesh & pretending to be a poem.

A Desert Highway Is the Best Kind of Highway When You Are Twenty-Four & Helping a Friend Move Across the Country to Get Married

Imagine we had another chance.
Two more hours, say,

or whole new lifetime.
Another road trip to Phoenix,

all hand jobs & toll roads.
Imagine the green-eyed babies

we might have made.
Imagine the mountains

turned upside down.
The distance inside out.

The desert underwater.
South American novelists

would have written of us,
this idea of us I'm inventing

in which you are sand
& I am sun, you are sky

& I cannot breathe.
We made the right decision,

we did, & regret is the worst
kind of lie. Still, the difference

between love poem & elegy
is only timing. Imagine—

here I mean *remember*—
I-10's dawn-pink asphalt

stretched ahead like a river
of possibility.

Morning riding into view,
our voices hoarse

from singing "Tainted Love"
with the windows down,

hands tangled in each other's zippers
at 65 mph. We were so young.

Already the heat was unbearable.

When the Topic Turns to Crazy Things
We've Done for Work

I pull out the time when as a vet assistant
I held the head of a purebred English bulldog
while the vet masturbated it. This was for
an insemination we'd do later, the pair
of dogs having failed to connect
on their own despite several tries. The male
was happy enough to hump the doctor's gloved hand,
& if this isn't already a good enough story,
the punchline is that the dog finished
with more, um, enthusiasm than we expected.
Enough of the results wound up
in the test tube to get the job done, yes, but also
plenty landed on the vet's face. I worked
for this vet my senior year of high school,
ten hours a week at minimum wage;
the rest of the time I looked for someone
to make out with. I haven't changed
that much, I guess. It wasn't all pitiful.
There was K., whose hair was the same color
as her eyes. S., whose mother had all the cats.
A., who was kind of mean,
but I was eighteen & willing
to put up with most anything
in exchange for someone's hands
on my face & a tongue in my mouth.
I learned to spin blood & analyze
fecal samples for parasites. Once
a whole family came in with a golden

retriever that had been hit by a truck.
We had no chance. They cried in the office
for an hour. I had not grown up with pets—
when our animals died it was usually
for meat, & I had never seen such grief.
I wish I could tell you it made me
a better person. When it happened,
with the bulldog, we all laughed,
even the vet. That's not the point
of the story. There isn't one,
I guess, it's just a thing that happened
after K. dumped me, before S. or A.,
& I drove home that night wondering
if I would be alone for the rest of my life.

Aubade with Junk Mail

I imagine a boy forever walking up a mountain to meet a girl:
a gravel path, bare December limbs. It's raining, foggy,
someone is in love, someone is pretending, someone
is taking what they can get. I imagine a boy alone,
maybe sad, or claiming sadness like a badge,
a thing to be proud of. He waits on a bench by a fountain
in the middle of the night. No one knows
where he is, which pleases him. The water
moves & moves. It's a trick. There's a pump
somewhere beneath the surface of things,
so much hidden machinery to keep it all flowing.
The pipes are faint between the world we see
& the world that is, between what we imagine
& what we remember. I imagine the boy again,
now holding hands with another girl.
I imagine them laughing as they walk
through a neighborhood like this one.
They have stayed up all night for this moment.
For this life. A sidewalk, a blue house,
motion lights, a dog barking on another block.
The mail is here, but there's never anything good.
No letters. Not from the sidewalk girl, not
from the girl on the mountain who long ago
moved to a house by the gulf,
a cabin on a cape in the path of all those hurricanes,
she always was wiser than the boy, who still dreams
of a canyon in springtime, dappled with green sunlight
& waiting to be filled. If there were a letter
what might it say? Something about the elastic

& boundless capacity of the human heart
for love. Or nothing. It might say nothing:
an inkless sheet of stationery, light blue
& smelling of a distant perfume. Crushed flowers, say.
Or rain, fog, wet branches. A winter morning.

Pastoral with Rosé

I assume my life remains on a trajectory
toward a 1983 Riuniti on Ice commercial:
shrimp cocktail & chilled sweet wine on a patio
with a crowd of well-dressed friends.
These beautiful people. What having money
must look like. I imagine the jokes
I would make, how they would earn me
praise from the assembled wives & husbands,
I imagine myself easy to envy. To be happy
ought to be enough. It is not. One must be
seen being happy, one's happiness
the sort of thing that sparks arguments
between couples on their drives home,
neither of them honest about the source
of their irritation as they bicker
& fall quiet, their silence in the darkness
a kind of privacy. I am entirely invested
in this nonexistent Amorak. I imagine him
lingering outside long after everyone has left
as cigar smoke & perfume melt into the dusk
& ice fades to water in copper buckets.
Chorus frogs. Fireflies. I imagine him lonely.
I pity him, though surely he has more sex than I do,
has hair he doesn't have to think about,
a slimmer waist, stronger calves.
The moon rises. He vanishes.
I am left to wonder how he pronounces our name.
Is it the same? Or have I been saying
it wrong all these years, every version
of myself in disarray, even on my own tongue?

Luminescence

They're converting chicken excrement into energy,
all that phosphorous, light-bearer, giver of life—
one percent of all our body weight, no wonder
you shimmer when the air touches your flesh.
You sleep for a dozen days, a dozen more,
wake in my arms under winter's morning star.
In Hamburg, Germany, in 1699, an alchemist
turned evaporated piss into this cold fire
while looking for the philosopher's stone:
all our achievements born in the body, inspired
by the same hunger to turn lead to gold.
This is the great work. This has been going on
since God told Adam about the stone
but would not let him touch it, the story goes,
& no legend has ever made more sense
as an explanation of the human condition.
Each element some blend of hot, cold,
wet, dry. Rearrange the balance
& everything changes. Something new
is born. Maybe even gold. We need time, desire,
an understanding of how one shape
attaches to the next. Too much of anything
kills what it touches, creates water where no fish swim,
surface abloom above all that darkness.
How have we ended up here? One accident
after another, that's how. Imagine
striking that first match—
the scratch, the hiss, the sudden flame
you hoped for. I have never felt so lonely.

A Scene Destined for the Cutting Room Floor

The director eats can after can of SpaghettiOs
& demands more vulnerability.
The leading man has dysentery.
We all have dysentery.
No doubt this scene
is intended to explain
something essential
about the nature of life.
It also must keep the plot moving.
It has been rewritten six times
by eight writers. No one cares.
Someone spent hours
sewing these curtains
in the name of authenticity.
No one cares. A man with strong
hands arose early
to build this floor
we're standing on
so carelessly.
We've gotten so much right.
Our ad–libbing has never been better.
The light is magnificent.
We are hitting our marks.
But this is how it goes.
It is, in the end,
beautiful enough
but extraneous.

PUNCHLINES

Dad Jokes

You're rolling your eyes already.
Nice to meet you, Rolling Your Eyes
Already, I'm Dad; did you hear
what the zero said to the eight?
Nice belt & also *I'm gonna need to see your passport.*
If you're American in the living room
& European in the bathroom
what are you in the airport holding cell?
Don't worry, I've got like a million of these.
You seem to have an allergic reaction on your skin
but let's not make any rash decisions,
health care is complicated. What
did the fish say when it swam into a wall?
What do you call an immigrant with no eyes?
What do you call someone
threatening to blow up Jewish daycares?
Why do I take peanut butter
on my morning commute?
I think you know. Sandwich
walks into a bar, bartender says
sorry we don't make gay wedding cakes
here. Secretary of Education
walks into a school, bartender says
sorry we're so poor. Chicago walks
into America, bartender says
look at all those black people killing each other.
Electoral college walks into November,
bartender says thank you for saving
us from Chicago. I'm starting to dislike

this bartender. You might think this
isn't funny. I get it. I didn't like the beard
either, until it grew on me.
At some point I came to understand
my job was to make the world
more bearable for my children.
It's possible I was wrong & anyway
I don't think I'm very good at it.
You pick your battles, you pick your nose,
but you can't pick yourself up
off the ground in a cloud of teargas.
No one's laughing. I'm not laughing.
I have broken my arm in several places,
now I'm thinking it would be best
not to go to those places anymore.

Poems Autocorrects to Porns

which doesn't make sense because isn't porn like soup
or fog? But maybe so are poems, maybe
we're all tangled in the effort to give language
to our body's cravings: the human condition,
in other words. My phone thinks
it knows what I want. Maybe it does.
My phone can talk to clouds after all,
can turn my voice into zeroes & ones
& put it back together on the other side
of the continent, in my brother's ear
when I call to tell him a joke I heard
about the lonely Cheerio. There is no punch line,
is the punchline, & I don't get to hear
him laugh so often as I used to.
He calls me brother, & we hang up
& go on with our lives, I'm wondering
what my search history says about me—
that's not true. I know exactly
what it says, but I'm not sure
how embarrassed I should be. For years
our favorite was about a fuzzy dog,
a really, really, really fuzzy dog
who wins a series of fuzzy-dog contests,
until finally, at the most prestigious
fuzzy-dog contest in the universe,
one last judge takes one look at the fuzzy dog
& says, "Doesn't look that fuzzy to me,"
in other words, the human condition.
The point isn't the dog anyway,

it's to make the telling take as long
as possible. My brother was always
better at that. Some comedian had a bit
about how many porn movies he'd seen
the first two minutes of. Similarly, I have
read the titles of many poems. I remember
the set-up of many jokes. It's so easy
to get lost in the other words, is the point,
to say one thing & mean another,
easy to see how such a mistake could happen.

To the Dads at Buffalo Wild Wings Watching the Tigers Game on a Monday Afternoon in April

It's too loud because we're too old.
The beer is light, the sauce mild.
Our sons have no patience
for this sport. Our wives
have only patience.
Our parents are dying.
Our team is losing,
has lost a dozen times already,
the star pitcher never
having been the same
since someone published
a series of nude selfies
he took with his girlfriend.
We are pretty sure
this says something important
about hunger,
complacency. We keep
starting sentences
with "I'm older now
than he was when ..."
On our separate drives home
we will chew gum
to cleanse our breath;
we will forget to pick up
the dry cleaning.
We lose track of the score,
blame the bullpen,
over-tip the servers,

we expect a kind
of sympathy we have not
earned. This is what it looks like
to have inherited the earth.

Half-Life with Bumper Stickers

Bumper sticker: My Target list includes a nose-hair trimmer.
This is everything I need to know
about which half of my life I'm in.
All atoms decay but some are less stable
along the way. (Bumper sticker.)
Should I measure by the life I've had so far
or by what lies ahead?
So much grieving, either way.
Coming soon: the death of everyone I've ever loved
plus my own, in no particular order.
In no sense have I come to terms with this.
I have already failed to hide
the mortality thing from my kids,
though I suppose the inevitable is not my fault.
Somewhere, amid all the visits to the children's museum
& *Dora the Explorer* & a million Happy Meals,
a great-grandparent lets go. A hamster.
A classmate's mother. People die
& continue dying; this is the least
profound thing I've ever written,
another terrible bumper sticker.
There's something pleasing
about measuring by halves,
my life a theoretical frog
hopping along a theoretical log
in a word problem, nearing the end
without ever reaching it. But theory
is not practice, & I cannot go back
to brace for the questions

I should have seen coming:
What if you die? What if I die?
Rejected bumper sticker:
If you eat your broccoli, you will live forever.
Eventually I settled on the best I could offer:
none of us is going to die for a very long time.
For a while—long enough—my kids believe me.
Then I believe they still believe me.
Then we all know it's a lie but agree
to pretend otherwise for as long as we can.
Bumper sticker: Life is one bumper sticker
after another. Think of words that might ease some pain,
drive them around hoping someone sees.

Amorak Autocorrects to Amoral

which surely comes as no surprise to anyone
in the town where I grew up. I hated
that place. All those two-story New Deal homes

laid out in grids between churches.
The town mall where we practiced baseball
in summer, football in fall,

learning early the value of muscle
& God: a prayer before every game.
I've never felt so vulnerable, my bowed head

a lie. We had moved there
from 700 miles away & I always knew
I would leave. My first girlfriend

dumped me because of God.
She was right. Our mailman stopped by
to witness to my mother

about the nature of love.
My friends slipped New Testaments
into my bag at sleepovers.

This isn't the whole story.
I still don't listen very well
though it's not true

that I hated it there.
That girl did teach me to kiss,
after all, the possibilities

of tongue & the small miracle
of holding hands in the dark;
she taught me to believe

in innocence. Each spring, the river
flooded. So much time has passed
& now I watch my own daughter

ignoring me. I wonder
who she will break up with & why.
Where will she feel at home?

I drove her through that town once
on our way to the ocean.
Predictably, everything was smaller

than I remembered, the whole
experience less meaningful
than I hoped. An entire town

in need of a fresh coat of paint.
If God was still there,
we did not see him.

What Happened

was my mother called me. She never calls
me. I should say rarely. Instead she waits
for me to call her. I never. I should say
rarely. I should say sometimes. Should say
I do, I mean I do, but maybe not as often.
I am not good at being her son. Not as good
as I should—she called because
my aunt has leukemia. Her sister. My aunt
who lives one hour and forty-eight minutes
away, according to internet directions
and whom I have not seen in two years.
One year? Maybe three. Something like that.
Leukemia is blood cancer. Is bone
marrow cancer. Is cancer that renders
the body's infection-fighting white blood
cells ineffective. Is malignant. Is progressive.
Is treatable, sometimes, sort of, maybe.
She was tired. We're all tired, most of us
most of the time, but my aunt's tired was
different. Was because of something.
She could tell. The body knows
these things, sometimes, but she wanted
to hear the word. She asked. The answer
was—I told you already. I'm not doing
very well. I am better at looking
for metaphors; leukemia is not
a metaphor. It's hard to hear. We're better off
not talking about it. This isn't true at all.
Listen. My mother called. Called again.

I answered, I answered. I have little
to say. Treatment has started. No one
knows if it will work. None of this—
but that's what happened.
      Is still happening.

Hey, Everybody, We're Invited to a Cookout!
—a hot dog, excitedly, on a T-shirt my kids
gave me for Father's Day

My eyes are failing me for the first time—
there is a distance at which words are too close
to read. Is this the beginning of the end
of being able to lie to myself? Or, the body's
way of suggesting there are things I'm better off
not knowing. Once, a few summers
after high school, some friends & I
went to Florida without telling another
friend we were going. He found out
by calling all of our homes every day
until someone's mother broke. I should
probably feel bad about it still, but it
sounds worse than it was. Or it's worse
than it sounds, I can't remember which.
He should have left it alone, but that's
not realistic. We can't stand not to know.
A nice day. A decent meal. The company of others.
It's all we really want, in the end, a few
such moments during our time in this world.
That's why commercials
are set on patios & back decks,
twilight & the clinking of glasses.
Laughter & a slow fade. It's a lifestyle
they're selling, all we need is the right
products. The appearance of happiness
is happiness. This is the premise
of all those churches in the town

where I grew up. The image
of God is God. The declaration
of salvation is salvation. Who
wouldn't want to share the good news?
The phone rings. It's an invitation. Tell the others.

All Those Boomerangs I Had as a Kid Never Came Back, but I Did Learn to Juggle Once

My son was in the appliance race
between innings tonight,
one of those minor-league traditions
in pursuit of hilarity & a small prize.
He was the water heater. His first move
was to knock over the dryer, which earned
him some applause, but the water-heater costume
is tall & thin & difficult to run in. He
could not catch the washing machine
despite a dive toward the finish line.
It made SportsCenter once when some kid fell down,
he said. *That was my goal.* My wife's father
made her a crayon costume one Halloween,
a carefully crafted painted tube, a colored
pointy hat. He refused to make armholes.
Would ruin the whole look, he said.
So my wife's sister had to carry her bag
& ring all the doorbells, which worked okay
until a door opened in a hurry
& knocked my future wife into the bushes
beside some stranger's porch, unable
to steady or catch herself. For a long time
I thought of this story as a cautionary tale
about aesthetics. About form vs. content.
But now I think it's about how we're always
choosing things that make no sense. As a species,
we are truly awful at changing our minds,
even in the face of overwhelming evidence;

once a thing is thought, that thing is real,
a lesson about metaphor, a reminder
that no matter what we're after,
king-sized Snickers or *SportsCenter* highlight
or merely a mild sense of achievement,
gravity wins in the end. We balance
until we cannot. We fall until we land.

American Prayer

Some parents on Facebook this morning are wondering whether it's truly PJ day at the elementary school. Trust but verify & all that, which is something a president once said about international diplomacy or maybe the motto of a newspaper, I forget, but if your mother says she loves you, check it out, right? What happens if our children wind up alone in their Hogwarts robes, their stegosaurus fleeces & sloth slippers, classmates clad in the usual: jeans, T-shirts, sweaters & soccer jerseys, track pants & armor-plated backpacks? Perhaps a valuable lesson in how we are ultimately on our own. In the limits of what we can prepare for. In how we know when things have gone disastrously awry. We have children & hope for the best, my god, but that's not always what we get. *Let 'em wear pajamas,* someone's father posts, *what's the worst*—though he doesn't mean it, we know the answer. Spring is weeks away but it's cold & the sidewalks are winter-slick: half-melted, refrozen, dangerous. *Bundle up*, we beg, & our children tumble into the sky of a new day, ceramic, shatterproof, & dressed for dreaming.

Badger Buries Entire Cow Carcass
—The New York Times, April 3, 2017

I accidentally freaked out my students the other day
when one mentioned that, working on an essay about dead dads,
she'd had little luck Googling stats about death rates among dads.
That's because the stat is 100 percent, I said,
& my students gasped in a was-he-joking-I-guess-
that-wasn't-really-a-joke-I-can't-believe-he-said-that way.
They don't always seem young & I don't always feel old,
but there we were. My father is still alive, a sentence
only temporarily true; I was taught that a sentence
represents a complete thought, which seems impossible,
as if one could pinpoint the beginning or end of thought,
but the stat is 100 percent. A semicolon
suggests a sort of equality between two independent clauses,
I used one in the previous sentence because I could not
bear to end the thought so soon. It's a lot of work,
being alive & continuing to think in the face of certain death,
but that's the job. I was reading about this badger
scientists recorded burying a calf carcass. It took four days.
Now *that's* a complete sentence. Badger sees cow,
badger thinks, *Bury cow,* badger buries cow. Period.
I watched some of the video. This badger was serious.
How long can a badger live on a carcass' measure
of rotting beef? I'm guessing a year, maybe eighteen months.
You know that badger figured it had won the meat lottery
when it found this cow, left by scientists studying
scavenger behavior. Eventually we are all scavengers;
the stat is 100 percent. I sent the video to my father.
He sent back a link to a *New Yorker* article

about nostalgia. How we sometimes miss
things that never existed or are not yet gone.
I miss more than I can say. What would you do
if you were walking through the desert of your allotted days
& came across everything you ever wanted?
Eat what you can. Bury the rest.

Driving Home After Thanksgiving, We Learn That Ariana Grande Has Been Named Artist of the Year

Dark when we depart, dark when we arrive—
in between we listen to pop music,
complain about the neverendingness of Indiana,
pretend we are not bored of our own company.
This is the nature of time: every moment
of life a metaphor for all the others.
Ariana Grande played Cat in that show
the kids used to watch, played the same
character in a second show, this new incarnation
peacocking up the most attention-hungry traits
of the original: the arc of the self bends
toward caricature. She also sings
about wanting less talk & more touch,
a Nobel-worthy sentiment for sure, & I'm only
mostly kidding. I can't say aloud
how these lyrics rumple my blood
because my kids are here & they have
no idea how much I think about desire,
how much I desire. I offer instead a half-assed diatribe
on "Material Girl" & self-determination,
the passage of time & the corporatization of music.
My thesis & all my supporting evidence
are things I assume or do not quite remember.
My wife is rolling her eyes. My kids have tuned out.
I am alone. I have been driving so long
my body will still feel in motion days from now.

One day Ariana Grande will play a concert
where a bomb goes off & people die. Ariana Grande
will reveal herself as a kind & sympathetic human
in the aftermath. We do not know any of this yet
though we should probably see it coming.
We are quiet for miles. Green signs count down
our remaining journey. Out of nowhere
my daughter asks *What would happen if someone built a city*
but forgot to make roads to connect it to anywhere else?
People would eventually find it, I say.
Which is sort of an answer. Sort of a prayer.

Doing Yard Work in Michigan, I Recall Visiting Ground Zero the Week the United States Invaded Iraq

When our neighbor's aging catalpa tree comes down, it's almost sure
to land on our daughter's room. So it goes.
Bean tree, cigar tree, *Catalpa speciosa*—
long planted outside its natural range
because we like the way it looks & crave the shade.
We make most choices thinking ourselves eternal,
not subject to the usual cellular decay
or granted special dispensation via some kind of god.
Turritopsis dohrnii—the immortal jellyfish—
has theoretically achieved this state but in practice
it's almost sure to succumb to disease or predator.
So it goes. My daughter was three months old
when we visited New York. We wanted to join
the protests but decided this was not a thing new parents did
so instead took a ferry to Liberty Island—
the statue closed because of terrorism,
we sat in the sun & asked a stranger to take our picture.
Later we walked from Battery Park
to where the towers no longer stood:
a field of dirt, a few men in construction vests,
windows plywooded on condemned buildings nearby,
soon to come down themselves. Our daughter in her stroller,
one sock lost somewhere along the way & the sun going down,
we were failing to keep her warm, to make sense
of this experience, to grieve or gain
or feel much of anything. We had the sense

these were Schrodinger's towers: there, not there.
To be alive is to be dying. So it goes. I don't
know what we expected. If I remember right,
which I do not, we met a friend
for Tibetan food in the Village that evening,
then took a cab back to our hotel & made love
while our daughter slept in a portable crib.
This tree is a problem but for now I'm trimming
the Chinese privet—*Ligustrum sinense*—that separates
us from our neighbors. It's easy work,
yields visible progress & a sense of achievement,
but there's little music in it. Does it count
as having visited a place if we returned unchanged?
If we did not buy a single souvenir?

Putting the Fun in Fungible

Some comedian has a one-liner about kids
being sent here to replace us. Nothing
is funny anymore. Some comedian.
Sometimes looking at my son
is like looking in a time-traveling mirror:
me at whatever age you have to be
to think a face lasts forever.
My son is handsomer than I am,
though I'm biased in his favor,
also he's probably a nicer person,
so an upgrade for the world in the long run,
unless I bollocks it up for him. He carries
the dank sock smell of a 12-year-old
in a hurry & I don't get to decide
when or whether he'll outgrow it. Time
is one of those soul-sucking office jobs
where they make you train your replacement
before they freeze your passwords
& send a security guard
to watch you pack the family photos
on your desk, escort you
from the building. There's not much to it:
help with homework until the homework
surpasses my abilities. Play catch
until twilight, wrestle in the living
room until he beats me. The work
would be pretty straightforward
if I weren't so emotionally attached.
I'd like to think I'd get more credit for caring

but I told you he was in a hurry. I still need
to teach him to drive, to do his own laundry,
to strike a match, all his fires still
to start, they're asking me to come
in early this morning to talk
about the future, I'm afraid there's no good
way to say this, they've decided to go
in a new direction.

Lifespan of a Deer

*The life span of a whitetail deer can be from 6 to 14 years in captivity.
In the wild, the majority of deer don't make it to that age because of
disease, hunting, and automobile collisions. The average life span for
wild whitetail deer is 4½ years.*
       —Journal of Wildlife Management

Three times in the past two days I drove past a dead doe
buckled & bloody against the median on the East Beltline.
My son asked how she got there. All the way to the middle,
he meant, gesturing at the many lanes of traffic
she must have negotiated, until she didn't.
I don't know, I said, maybe there weren't as many
cars when she tried to cross. I am forever
telling my kids I don't know.
Thirteen years ago, a family trip, touring
a castle; the guide pointed out
the suite a sultan had built for his mother
in the fifteenth century. My daughter
asked where the mother was right now
since we were tromping through her room.
She died, I said, though surely I found some gentler way
to phrase it, & my daughter said, Oh, that's sad,
& foolishly I felt her sadness
seemed out of proportion to the moment
so I said, It was a long time ago,
as if time's passage makes anything less sad. The next time
I drive on the East Beltline, I expect the deer
will be gone. As a society, we have gotten pretty good
at removing carcasses from public view.

When I was twenty-three & certain
of so much more than I am now, I watched a deer
walk into the water & swim three hundred yards
to the opposite shore of a lake in Alabama.
I spent the whole time sure I would see her drown
but she made it, despite a body
in no way built for swimming, all spindly limb
& top heavy. That deer is dead now,
it is certain, & that's sad, or it isn't,
I don't know any way to say such a thing
that is both gentler & not a lie.
These words are the words I have, is what I mean,
& it's okay if it's sad sometimes,
& I will protect you until I cannot
& I will want to for so much longer than that.

Childhood Goes Kaleidoscope, Kaleidoscope, Kaleidoscope, Gun

We keep waiting to wake up & know what we're doing;
we've learned to be grateful
for any colored shard of glass

not shaped like a bullet.

We are driving in a blizzard (not a metaphor,
we could die, I have a lot of responsibility
here) & our daughter

is telling us a ghost story, we're listening
for any clues to the riddle
that is her mind at 15—her life

has ceased to revolve
around us. There are so many
bullets, we've learned
not to take these small moments for granted.

In this story, the father
of the children of her Sims character
came to visit, refused to leave.
She built a tiny room, lured him in, deleted the door.

Thirty game-days later, he died.
The story takes a long time to tell,

our son keeps interrupting

to sing "We Got the Beat"
& talk about his plans
for his new AirSoft gun with the biodegradable ammo.

Everything is so dangerous (there
are no metaphors), it's our fault
for giving him what he wanted:

this world, its shattered edges. He has 2,000 pellets,
a freshly charged battery,
a friend to shoot. What more

could a boy desire? She likes
having the ghost around,
she says, better now than when he was alive,

& this sounds like a mostly okay ending,
probably all we can ask.

In Michigan, When the Season's First Snow
Explodes Upon Us Like a Star

after Brigit Pegeen Kelly

My son & I go out to build a snowman
but it is windy & more work
than we imagined. Cold & bored, we come in
for hot chocolate but we are out of hot chocolate.
He drifts downstairs to his PlayStation,
I'm at the window watching our headless
creation do nothing. My son named him
Stick Arm Wild Eyes, renamed him
Unfinished No Arms Sorry Dude. Every conversation
with my kids starts with one of them asking
is the world really this shitty & me saying:
Yes. Yes, it is, but—& there things fall apart.
I do not know how to rescue my answer.
Outside, the wind. Outside, the whiteness.
We do not have a fireplace,
we pay a monthly bill for our warmth.
It is my birthday. I am past middle age:
more lies behind than ahead. I am not asking
anyone to feel sorry for me,
we're fine. We're better than fine.
My book, tented on the table beside my chair:
Gailey's *A Field Guide to the End of the World.*
The last lines I read: "The body is a place of violence.
Wolf teeth, amputated hands." Yes.
I was named after a wolf, sort of,
& I've been mispronouncing my own name
ever since. We took out two clementines

to use for eyes, thinking big orange eyes
would be funny. This is a fruit we created,
seedless, sweet, easy to peel. Popular
around the holidays. By "we" I mean whoever
is in charge of such things, bending the world
to our taste. My son is playing Madden
& singing Christmas songs, loudly. My daughter
is yelling downstairs for him to shut up.
The weather is picking up, though I guess
that's always true. Yes, this is the world.
Yes, I am sorry about that. We left
the clementines on the porch steps.
We never made the head, so never needed
eyes. The snow closes over them.
It's okay. We're fine. We are all unfinished.
My son is still singing. I cannot tell
how much we are alike. A snowman
without a head is not a snowman:
two stacked & lopsided spheres.
Battered globes. Misshapen hearts.

NOTES

"Fairy Tale" ("I cannot wear my father's body") is after Tanya Grae's poem "Fairy Tale."

All three "Fairy Tale" poems draw inspiration from Jo McDougall's poem "Fairy Tale."

"Looking at Men" is after Iliana Rocha's poem "Looking at Women."

The title "Hey, Everybody, We're Invited to a Cookout!" is from a Charles Barsotti *New Yorker* cartoon (reprinted on a T-shirt my kids gave me for Father's Day).

"In Michigan, When the Season's First Snow Explodes Upon Us Like a Star" draws inspiration from Brigit Pegeen Kelly's poem "Song."

"FMK" and many of the other poems in this collection are heavily influenced by the poems in Maggie Smith's collection *Good Bones*.

The quoted lines "The body is a place of violence. / Wolf teeth, amputated hands" are from Jeannine Hall Gailey's poem "Introduction to the Body."

The poem "Driving Home After Thanksgiving, We Learn That Ariana Grande Has Been Named Artist of the Year" paraphrases Grande's song "Into You."

"A Dog Barks, Someone Eats a Watermelon, a Car Drives Away" is a quotation from Edan Lepucki's essay "Literary Fiction Is a Genre: A List," published by *The Millions* on October 22, 2012.

ACKNOWLEDGMENTS

I am grateful to the editors of the journals where many of these poems first appeared, sometimes in slightly different form or under different title:

Academy of American Poets' Poem-a-Day, March 20, 2019: "We Were All Odysseus in Those Days"

Alaska Quarterly Review: "Driving Home After Thanksgiving, We Learn That Ariana Grande Has Been Named Artist of the Year"

American Literary Review: "Doing Yard Work in Michigan, I Recall Visiting Ground Zero the Week the United States Invaded Iraq"

American Poetry Review: "Childhood goes kaleidoscope, kaleidoscope, kaleidoscope, gun"

Apple Valley Review: "To the Dads Watching the Tigers Game at Buffalo Wild Wings on a Monday Afternoon in April," "A Scene Destined for the Cutting Room Floor," and "Nocturne with Overdue Books"

Baltimore Review: "In the Final Months of My Parents' Marriage"

Barstow & Grand: "All Those Boomerangs I Had as a Kid Never Came Back, but I Did Learn to Juggle Once" and "Lifespan of a Deer"

Beech Street Review: "Captain Picard Teaches My Son to Throw a Football"

Bloodroot: "A Desert Highway Is the Best Kind of Highway When You Are Twenty-Four & Helping a Friend Move Across the Country to Get Married"

Cider Press Review: "Luminescence"

Columbia Poetry Review: "What happened"

Cotton Xenomorph: "The Girl on the Unicycle"

decomP: "Fairy Tale [We built a barn]," The World as We Have Invented It," and "The Seventh Anniversary Is Salt & I Do Not Know the Gift for That"

Four Way Review: "FMK" and "Badger Buries Entire Cow
        Carcass"
Golden Walkman Magazine: "Aubade with Junk Mail"
Gold Wake Live: "Elegy for Dr. Spock" and "Fred Flintstone &
        George Jetson"
Guesthouse Lit: "A Primer"
Gulf Coast: "Dad Jokes"
Iron Horse Literary Review: "In Michigan, When the Season's
        First Snow Explodes Upon Us Like a Star"
JARFLY: "Still Life with Laughtrack"
Love's Executive Order: "American Prayer"
Pithead Chapel: "A Dog Barks, Someone Eats a Watermelon, a Car
        Drives Away"
Quiddity: "Steven Keaton & Dan Conner & Bob Saget & Alan
        Thicke & Both of My Two Dads" and "Pa"
Rise Up Review: "Yes, And"
Rogue Agent: "You're All Why Are We Here & I'm All Because
        of Sex & You're All You're Not as Funny as You
        Think You Are & I'm All I'm Not Joking" and
        "Amorak Corrects to Amoral"
Rubbertop Review: "The Song & Dance Comic Teaches Method
        Acting"
The Rumpus: "Ward Cleaver & Mike Brady & Fred MacMurray
        & Dick Van Patten"
Rust + Moth: "Fairy Tale [I cannot wear my father's body—]"
The Saint Ann's Review: "When the Topic Turns to Crazy Things
        We've Done for Work"
The Shallow Ends: "Hey, Everybody, We're Invited to a
        Cookout!"
The Southern Review: "Road Trip," "I Am Not Arnold
        Schwarzenegger," "Pastoral with Rosé," "Fairy Tale
        [My father cuts off his thumb]"
Sporklet: "Poems Autocorrects to Porns"
Stirring: "Half-Life with Bumper Stickers"
Tahoma Literary Review: "The World Is Full of Dogs Without
        Collars"

Third Point Press: "Prayer for What I Do Not Want"
Tinderbox Poetry Journal: "Putting the Fun in Fungible"
TYPO: "Looking at Men"
Yes, Poetry: "When a Poet Writes *Afterward* You Know It
        Means"

"Yes, And" was reprinted on the website of *Bullets into Bells: Poets & Citizens Respond to Gun Violence.* "We Were All Odysseus in Those Days" also appears in the Norton Critical Edition of Emily Wilson's translation of *The Odyssey* (W.W. Norton, 2020).

THANK YOU

I owe so much to so many for helping me make these poems. Thank you to Erin Elizabeth Smith, Jeremy Michael Reed, and the amazing team at Sundress Publications for ushering this collection into the world. Thank you to Maggie Smith for your insightful editorial eye on an early draft. Thank you to Traci Brimhall for your inspiration and feedback. Thank you to my homie and collaborator W. Todd Kaneko. Thank you to Chris Haven and the rest of the Poet's Choice gang—Aaron Brossiet, Christina Olson, Jean Prokott, Judy Halebsky, Dean Rader, Brian Clements, Amy McInnis, Ashley Cardona, and Brian Komei Dempster—for your words. Thank you to my colleagues in the Grand Valley State University Writing Department for your support. Thank you to Malcolm, Marilyn, and Silas. And thank you, thank you, thank you to Ellen Schendel for all these years of being parents together and for tolerating even my worst jokes.

This book was completed with the assistance of a fellowship from the National Endowment for the Arts.

ABOUT THE AUTHOR

Amorak Huey teaches writing at Grand Valley State University in Michigan. He is the author of three previous books of poetry and two chapbooks, as well as co-author with W. Todd Kaneko of the textbook *Poetry: A Writer's Guide and Anthology*.

OTHER SUNDRESS TITLES

The Valley
Esteban Rodriguez
$16

To Everything There Is
Donna Vorreyer
$16

nightsong
Ever Jones
$16

JAW
Albert Abonado
$16

Bury Me in Thunder
syan jay
$16

Gender Flytrap
Zoë Estelle Hitzel
$16

Boom Box
Amorak Huey
$16

Afakasi / Half-Caste
Hali F. Sofala-Jones
$16

What Nothing
Anna Meister
$16

Hood Criatura
féi hernandez
$16

Maps of Injury
Chera Hammons
$16

Lessons in Breathing Underwater
HK Hummel
$16

Dead Man's Float
Ruth Foley
$16

Blood Stripes
Aaron Graham
$16

Arabilis
Leah Silvieus
$16

Marvels
MR Sheffield
$20

CPSIA information can be obtained
at www.ICGtesting.com
Printed in the USA
JSHW041608010521
14050JS00003B/11